GW00707336

The Weather on the Moon

Robin Thomas spent most of his working life in an engineering company in Reading having qualified as a chemical engineer at Birmingham University. While still employed, he obtained a degree in English Studies from the then Polytechnic of North London, followed by an MA in Victorian Poetry at the Open University and an MA in Writing Poetry at Kingston University. He is married with a daughter and lives in Caversham.

The Weather on the Moon

Robin Thomas

TWO
RIVERS
PRESS

By the same author

A Fury of Yellow (Eyewear, 2016)
Momentary Turmoil (Cinnamon, 2018)
A Distant Hum (Cinnamon, 2021)
Cafferty's Truck (Dempsey and Windle, 2021)

Also by Two Rivers Poets

David Attwooll, *The Sound Ladder* (2015)
Charles Baudelaire, *Paris Scenes* translated by Ian Brinton (2021)
William Bedford, *The Dancers of Colbek* (2020)
Kate Behrens, *Man with Bombe Alaska* (2016)
Kate Behrens, *Penumbra* (2019)
Kate Behrens, *Transitional Spaces* (2022)
Conor Carville, *English Martyrs* (2019)
David Cooke, *A Murmuration* (2015)
David Cooke, *Sicilian Elephants* (2021)
Tim Dooley, *Discoveries* (2022)
Jane Draycott, *Tideway* (re-issued 2022)
Jane Draycott & Lesley Saunders, *Christina the Astonishing* (re-issued 2022)
Claire Dyer, *Interference Effects* (2016)
Claire Dyer, *Yield* (2021)
John Froy, *Sandpaper & Seahorses* (2018)
James Harpur, *The Examined Life* (2021)
Maria Teresa Horta, *Point of Honour* translated by Lesley Saunders (2019)
Ian House, *Just a Moment* (2020)
Rosie Jackson & Graham Burchell, *Two Girls and a Beehive* (2020)
Gill Learner, *Chill Factor* (2016)
Gill Learner, *Change* (2021)
Sue Leigh, *Chosen Hill* (2018)
Sue Leigh, *Her Orchards* (2021)
Becci Louise, *Octopus Medicine* (2017)
Mairi MacInnes, *Amazing Memories of Childhood, etc.* (2016)
Steven Matthews, *On Magnetism* (2017)
Henri Michaux, *Storms under the Skin* translated by Jane Draycott (2017)

René Noyau, *Earth on Fire and other Poems* translated by Gérard Noyau
    with Peter Pegnall (2021)
James Peake, *Reaction Time of Glass* (2019)
James Peake, *The Star in the Branches* (2022)
Peter Robinson & David Inshaw, *Bonjour Mr Inshaw* (2020)
Peter Robinson, *English Nettles* (re-issued 2022)
Lesley Saunders, *Nominy-Dominy* (2018)
Lesley Saunders, *This Thing of Blood & Love* (2022)
Jack Thacker, *Handling* (2018)
Susan Utting, *Half the Human Race* (2017)
Jean Watkins, *Precarious Lives* (2018)

First published in the UK in 2022 by Two Rivers Press
7 Denmark Road, Reading RG1 5PA.
www.tworiverspress.com

ISBN 978-1-909747-97-5

1 2 3 4 5 6 7 8 9

Two Rivers Press is represented in the UK by Inpress Ltd
and distributed by Ingram Publisher Services UK.

Cover illustration and design by Sally Castle
Text design by Nadja Guggi and typeset in Janson and Parisine

Printed and bound in Great Britain by Severn, Gloucester

Acknowledgements

Thanks to my many friends on the poetry scenes in Reading, Bath and
elsewhere. Thanks are also due to the editors of the following in which
some of these poems previously appeared: *Agenda, Envoi, Orbis, Brittle
Star, Pennine Platform, The High Window, Poetry Scotland, South, Poetry
Salzburg Review, Stand, Rialto, The Interpreters House* and *North.*

For Mary and Caitlin

Contents

The Wonder of Art

Le Dejeuner Sur L'herbe, Éduoard Manet, 1862

The woman appears to be naked
and the men clothed. In fact,
the woman wears a bodystocking
and the men are naked although
artfully made up to look as if they're
dressed, like boulevardiers, perhaps
or flaneurs. The painter,
discretely employing artistic licence,
has painted the woman naked
and the men clothed.

The Treachery of Images

R. Magritte, 1929

Actually it *is* a pipe; it's the painting
that's the problem – pipes are found
not in pictures but in tobacconists,
the bulging pockets of sports jackets
and in racks in gentlemen's studies.

One such reaches for a briar
across a huge mahogany desk. He
can only just reach it. He could
do with a smaller desk. You can
see all this in my painting of it
que n'existe pas, for obvious reasons.

Skating

The ice is permanent. It extends
beyond sight, merging with the sky,
as solid, as impenetrable, as truth,
as true as skaters, as skates, as scarves,
gloves and warm hats, as scratches
in the surface, as the pale sun, which sinks,
to rise tomorrow for all we know.

Nothing beneath the ice that can be seen.
No fish, no monsters, no swirling
currents, no order, no realm of forms,
nothing to disturb the figures of eight,
the swooping curves, the glowing faces,
no reason to suppose

a thinness here, or over there,
under the looming trees, no reason
for a crack, a sudden absence above
and who knows what below.

Imperatives

The lion waited
while the creature came near,
then sprang,
clawing, biting, dragging,
until, shuddering, the animal
became a sack of food.

It lay down to digest its meal
and while it did so, ruminated:
'I need to eat. I can't eat grass.
This is how I get my food.
It's him or me. He's

my enemy: he would if he could
lie in wait and stab me
with his horns, he would
fast talk me into his herd
and they would surround
and trample me. He's
more primitive than me,
his kind out-breed mine.
They are ugly.
They are Other'.

Is it a mad, mad, mad, mad world?

Was Van Gogh mad? And did his paintings
emerge therefrom? Who can tell?
And who cares, except those whose living it is.

All painting is mad, if not for money.

To live is mad, if not to eat, or madly make.
Ask any ant or tiger.

The explosion of the universe is mad,
if not to keep exploding.

God is mad, unless he isn't there. Who would design
such sanity?

So Van Gogh, in his swirling yellows and light
and remade world, his try at priesthood, his self
incarceration, his ear and deadly aim was mad?

If so, thank God.

Horizons

Sean Scully, National Gallery, 2019

I could almost say I like him –
and I like him a lot and
what he has to say about art,
whatever that is –
more than his work.

I like him walking on a painting
made of sea and wet sand. I like
him on windows and doorways
that 'sweeten the bitterness of facades'.

I like his postures and gestures,
his ruined boxer's face, his crooked smile,
his outrageous confidence.

And yet, those patchworks and
patternings, those layers
piled each on each in black
and dirty oranges and yellow,
that sombre blue on blue,
the ever-retreating sea ...

Coming back

after Du Fu

They will not come back.
When they do, they will bring nothing
in porcelain bowls or stacked
in threes or tied with ribbons
in bundles like twigs, to fill our urn.
Just as well – it's already overflowing
like a lake teeming with absent fish.

Unmendable

after Philip Larkin 'The Mower'

The earth quaked, twice, enough for countless
rats, mice, insects, humans, hedgehogs, dogs
to be tossed away, leaving space for replacements
in due course.

Who knows what conversations, loves,
jokes, eatings, toils, arguments, murderous intents,
dreams, pursuits came to an end
in that moment.

They fought the rubble, the heat, the escaping gas,
bringing out body after concrete dust and
blood-smeared body, and, occasionally, something
crying, and newly orphaned.

No point being kind,
but you might as well be.

Productivity

Coachlined lustrous redyellowblue '57 Chevy,
scrapyard scavenged, blown straight eight powered,
towered on truck wheels bursting from arches,
forged by Weldurup's team of magicians
at South Highland Drive, Las Vegas, under
Steve Darnell's critical, mercurial eye,
snorts and thunders from the shop, ready
to swap itself for bundles of greenbacks from
cowboy-hatted, whooping, yee-haa-ing customers.

Meanwhile John – lately retired from Beech and Son,
manufacturers of water pump gaskets
for the motor vehicle and domestic appliance trades,
located in Cardiff Road industrial estate –
and his wife Janet walk under the leafiness
to Emmer Green, for some shopping,
a cup of coffee and perhaps something to eat.

Nature is smiling. She is satisfied
with their output: Cheyenne, Ethan,
Parker, Logan, Norma, Adeline,
Harper; Christopher, David and Emma.

Avenida Atlântica

When there's a gap
between the big cars
I'll run across
to the golden beach
by the dazzling sea
to fetch deckchairs,
towels and drinks
for the tanned girls,
the muscled boys.

Our Lord up there
looks far off and colourless
to me, not like
the picture by my bed.

I'll have to be careful
when I come back.
I'll be tired, like João
must have been.

Flood

after Ted Hughes

I drown in the thrumming flood,
in the ice-cold heat of ever rising waters.
Waterfowl eye me, creatures
on floating branches, on mountain tops,

peer at me, me out of place. I hurtle
to the edge of the streaming falls, fall
to join the bones of my brothers, sisters
and children. I go down
in the knowledge of my lastness.

There are games of competitive quoits

and races in the pool. Golfers
hit practice balls into the sea. Corporations
hold sensible discussions about plans for the future
around a long table in a stateroom and politicians
snipe at each other along the length of the deck. Amateurs
strive to reach grade eight and there are
rehearsals for *As You Like It* in one of the available halls. Enthusiasts
build a model of Manhattan in matchsticks. Couples
sit in lifeboats planning their children's future and the band
plays a selection of popular songs.

Species of Disappointment

and they get married but
turn over the page, and there's nothing:
no country walks, no carriage rides, no balls,
no minor gentry, no dangerous gypsies,
no thundering horses and best friends,
no clerics wearing ridiculous wide brimmed hats,
no charming nephews and nieces, no
bored and straying husbands,
no gout, no tuberculosis, nothing,

or the gangster is consumed in a blaze
of gasoline and there are no more
broads, violin cases and
exaggerated double-breasted suits, only
flickering credits,

or the major and minor journeys are
complete, the penultimate dissonance
resolved and the next note is
silent,

or the children have flown
leaving only an echoing house,
your career has run down to a clock
and there are only visits to places of interest,
the grandchildren on skype and weekday golf
(there's no nineteenth hole).

The Heinous Crime

being an update of Sonnet 19 for the 21st century

Oh space-time, blunt the orbit
of our sun, pluck our little earth from out
its steady rhythms so it
careen across the ether, its expiring days
sad and merry, hot and cold, then
hot, and hotter still until ... but
one thing only I beg of you – burn
not my love, that speck of dust
you could not assay in even
your most meticulous arithmetic.

Oh let her be! This gnat, this flea that lives
upon the gnat, which even the gnat can't see.
You will not listen? Then do your worst!
You cannot prevent that my love live
in my poor lines at least until
your flailing arm knocks our puny globe
off its hair-sprung balance.

Over the Hill

after the film *1917,* dir. S. Mendes

You're walking up the hill and pause to watch
spots in the sky, like distant flies, droning,
backwards and forwards, looking for something,
circling, playing with a new arrival
which soon drops away, fluttering and turning,
leaving a black smudge in the pale sky,
coming towards you but far away …
disappearing behind the hill …

Explodes in your face –
fuselage, wings, struts, wires,
propeller, oil, flames, splinters,
engine, flailing, spinning …

You wake. Was it a dream?

Answers

The serjeant takes the questions
from the supplicants,
places them on a silver tray
and takes them behind the curtain.

After a long silence come the replies:
'it is a bush, not a tree, although
with one twig more, it would be a tree'
'it is prose, although if the word "silver"
were deleted, it would be a poem'. 'Your finger
is finger for 5.7 centimeters from its tip,
then hand'. 'Australopithecus afarensis,
Homo habilis, Homo rudolfensis, Homo erectus,
Homo floresiensis and Homo heidelbergensis
are not found in heaven; Homo sapiens
alive prior to AD0 are assigned to Limbo,
as are Neanderthals'.

The serjeant frowns at a new question,
nevertheless places it on the tray,
takes it behind the curtain, from where
come sounds, and scrapings as of chairs.
The serjeant peers, goes in and reappears.
On his face surprise, perhaps dismay,
perhaps relief:

'That question, is inadmissible'

Reminiscing

i.m. Daisy Ellington, Duke Ellington and Billy Strayhorn

1. Daisy

The pain that now defines her
crumples the face laid on the pillow
beside hers. Unearthly chords
sound in their shared space. He will write
Reminiscing in Tempo, structuring
the new piece around those same
haunting sounds, inserting her
between the notes.

2. Billy

He cannot bear to be where he lies
gasping with spikes of pain which
Billy has converted into the lovely
Blood Count. Ellington will play this later
when he thinks no-one is listening.
He will play it straight, chorus after
unadorned chorus, inserting himself
between the notes.

Kinda Dukish

i.m. Duke Ellington and Billy Strayhorn

Ragtime, stride, creole, tailgate,
the marching bands of New Orleans,
Armstrong, Oliver, Henderson, birds
in the morning, the hoots of trains,
their slow, mesmeric rumble, the sidings,
and shunts, the back doors, a coffee order
at a roadside stop, the sound of the South,
of steamers' whistles on the Missouri,
Atlantic slap, the heave of Egypt, torrents
of Japanese rain. Huge ear, rule disdainer,
last minute man, inventor on the go.

Welcome shy Mr Strayhorn, let's see
what you have in your bag: schoolbooks,
essays, manuscripts, *Theory of Harmony*,
certificates, sketches, Debussy, a Pittsburgh
childhood, Ravel, your nimble hands,
the delicate precision of your ear.

Come, we'll catch the 'A' train
together.

Easy Does It

i.m. Lester Young and Count Basie

Weighed,
selected,
placed
there, there,
there

upon the thrust, the bounce, the throb
the steady throb, the movement,
always moving, always
going somewhere, always
almost there.

Above it a lightness,
a weighty trail of silver
alighting and lifting off,
skimming, skipping, going,
going somewhere, going
somewhere else.

Danger Zone

I. una selva oscura

I have come out to hear the dawn chorus
to the wood at the back of the house –
lit here only by a small torch, which casts
what feels like an unwelcome light on my
crunching, branchy route. I find an old
stump to sit on, and *click* – so. For a moment
I'm terrified: utter dark, only a scurrying
creature and my pulsing blood interfere

with the silence I came from and will go to.
I sense the nearness of the house, yearn for
the warm bed I've left. Is that a glimmer?
The birds think so and at once whip up
an air-filling broadside of warnings and messages
of such beauty it's surely meant for me.

This is a place where nature is here with me, not there with me in it.

II. Fire Flight

Does a butterfly exist if you don't see it? If it flapped its wings, they say, over the Amazon, the weather would change in China, assuming all three elements in the equation had being.

We unlocked the gate and went through into the wood, snapping our way to our favourite path, damp and yielding after light rain, rain which had left the parched leaves looking green, the air damp. So we moved forwards through the shadows, the spots of light and the varieties of green and brown, towards open land, continuing on our path. There we encountered tiny fluttering things, too busy to notice us, too lively for us to see properly, except sometimes they paused, as if proud of their dark pink and black wings or their glowing white ones. These, beautiful as they were, had no more than a week to affect the weather in New South Wales, to help or hinder the fire fighters.

The Fox Moth can remain a cocoon for five years, then it lives for a few weeks during which its reddish-brown wings may be seen. Catch it while you can! You'll never see the female, which flies only at night. A family of reddish-brown foxes visits our garden, to do, what? To delight us I think, which they do without cease – when we see them, we put down our breakfast spoons and observe them through the window, taking care not to move. Presumably they are influencing the weather on the moon.

I have boxes of time, stacked at one side of my study, taking up much needed space. One day, when they are all empty, I will throw them out. Oh, what will I do with the extra space?

III. He talks to the house that once he lived in

Do you remember when I fell out of the loft
and landed on the stairs?

> I remember it well. I tried to warn you.
> But couldn't.

Yes, there was a gap where the folding stairs came up.
I normally stepped across it but I was often

> Yes, you stepped into it, why or how I don't know.
> And down you went.

dreamy in those days, still am.
Next thing, I was sitting on the stairs below.

> I did my best to float you down,
> to soften the stairs.

I know you did. I sat there wondering
if I were still alive. I felt all my bones,

> I know, I could see you. I felt for you,
> I held my breath. I couldn't move.

but all seemed alright. I don't think
I even had a bruise. I don't think Mum and Dad

> They weren't in – they'd gone shopping -
> it was Saturday morning. They'd come back

were in, they didn't appear and I'm sure
I never mentioned it. My Mum

with those crusty rolls and tiny shrimps.
They'd have bought a half pint of them

would have fainted. I couldn't have borne it,
she'd seen me nearly die once already

and spend hours peeling them. Then
they'd put them in those thickly buttered rolls.

when I was two. I'd had pneumonia. She wasn't
allowed to come in: 'it would upset him'.

I don't remember that – it would have been
when you were living at my cousin's

*A moment in a life, the terrible stream of emotion, like light
from a distant star, otherwise nothing but time and space.*

IV. When I think about sanctuary,

I think of a place of safety in a whirling, dangerous world. But the word is only an idea. Thomas à Becket sought sanctuary in Canterbury Cathedral and like him, over the centuries, numerous people have sought safety in churches, in places away from the fighting, behind moats, under red crosses, in lifeboats, only to have their lives snatched away. Even if the place of safety is respected there is still the fear of the outside to which you must ultimately return – illness, pestilence, accident, the forces of evil – hover in the wings and if all else fails Death respects no sanctuary. Still the word has force, but in a less grand setting as in the sanctuary you have where you write – perhaps it's your study, or the kitchen table when everyone's gone to bed, or just your seat on a busy train – you can still find it among the buzzes and word noise around you, perhaps with the aid of ear plugs or defenders. Don't spend too long in sanctuary though. It's amongst the nuisance, noise, danger and delight of the world you need to be.

Sometimes I look up from my writing and hit a surge of sadness.

V. and loosing

That bridge spanning platforms one to fourteen,
designed for atom-gathering and fusing

of molecules for their efficient transportation
in unstoppable machines,

has lost its energy supply and lies stopped.
Now each atom becomes itself:

racing legs become legs, glancing eyes
become eyes worth looking at, briefcases

want to move on but pause and slowly
begin to smile.

There is no movement but a palpable
release of breath.

> *The shadows, which have been lengthening all afternoon,*
> *merge slowly into the stillness, when the mad growth all round*
> *freezes and sleeps, like the graves it is its business to reclaim.*

'The Strangeness of Modern Life'
(Edward Hopper)

America's Cool Modernism, Ashmolean Museum,
23 March to 22 July 2018

1. Precisionism

Charles Demuth et al

All roads are uninhabited.
The red brick and brick-red city
is empty even of roads;
and silence empties itself
across the great plain.

2. Which Way?

Martin Lewis

If the car,
which hesitates
at the wintry crossroads,
turns the wrong way
it will roar and slither into
starved and frozen
nothingness.

3. Dawn in Pennsylvania

Edward Hopper

The trolley is heaped with bags,
cases, trunks and boxes.
Those who pass through
are present, but not here.

Cape Cod Morning

Edward Hopper, 1950

A new day. Always new days. Always
this clear, untroubled, light.

No sound except the sough
of trees, of the wheat, the pipes' mutterings.

The house has bedrooms, living rooms, a dining room, a kitchen,
a breakfast nook, a mud room, a basement, a loft and a woman.

Nothing has happened since that day.

'But something
might happen today'.

The blind, indifferently installed, slides down
and stops, making a small noise.

'It might be today; the day is fresh and new.
Yesterday was a day of hope, but this is a new day'.

Triptych of the Virgin of Montserrat

Bartolomé Bermejo

– commissioned by merchant Francesco della Chiesa *c.* 1485

Packed into his ships: pigs and meal, barrels of water, wine, compass, maps, hacksaws, axes, awls, timber, rope, oakum, caulking irons, paint, arquebuses, bombards, petards, shot, broadswords and daggers, lances, wool and linen, flags, bales of tea, turmeric, pepper, silver, bibles, prayer books, angels, devils, purgatories, indulgencies, certainties, a promise: *Salve Regina!* If it be your wish, let my ventures be successful and in return I will honour you with a painted work by the best of our masters.

Bambino Vispo

Virgin adoring the Child in a landscape, Francesco Botticini,
c. 1475

Perfectly rounded hills, hornbeam, poplar, cypress, riverside
vineyards, stretching for ever in perfect peace – an earthly
paradise; a domed and heavenly sky.

Garments of red and gold, a cloak of bluest blue. Her
alabaster calm, her face the Form of female beauty. Her
pose an amaranthine reverence before the son of man.

At her feet the infant – naked, pink, all wriggling arms and
legs – the Type of itself.

> *Less*
> *of the adoration please.*
> *For heaven's sake*
> *just pick me up,*
> *I'm hungry.*

Room

The shelves in my room
are bursting with books,
from my youth,
from my pomp, of now.

My window looks down
to the garden next door,
where a cluster of birch trees -
shy slender brides –

marks the edge of a forest
of larch, pine, spruce,
oak, birch, aspen,
willow, lime …

Street Music

after Douglas Dunn, 'Loch Music'

Our road? Prokoviev maybe.
A symphony?

It's spring: the leaves
are impossibly green, birds
trill and scoot, squirrels hurry,
stop, peer, and flash away.

Summer will be fat and green,
autumn drip and flutter, winter
be echoey, inert and hard.

Spring, summer, autumn, winter,
you drive each day and the next
along our road to park and commute,
commute and return, too tired for life.

If you were not so tired, you might see,
if you looked in the mirror,

                       the yearnings,
the dark rhythms, the jumps and stabs,
the sprightly, curtailed melodies
of the Fifth, its seasons: Andante,
Allegro marcato, Adagio, Allegro
giocoso

Where Oscar and Pyotr liked to go

They loved this country, its sights, its scents,
its prospects, its stimuli, the ideas
spinning and whirling in the air.
They loved to ramble those paths
over the green hills, through charming villages
and by no means spurned
even the grey streets of the city,
its different sights and smells, all
meat and drink, herbs, spices and seasonings,
for what they made.

But best of all, they loved to walk
arm in arm
on the narrow ledge,
where the prettiest flowers grew,
by the yawning ravine. Narrow yes,
but perfectly safe, if you don't stumble.

Dance, Music

to be read to the tune of 'Stompin' at the Savoy'

it swings, the Benny Goodman band,
for dance, the lovers find it grand,
it is, the best known in the land.

it's got, a black arranger now,
his book, propels the band and how,
but no, he'll never take a bow.

then comes Teddy Wilson,
'Marxist Mozart', black,
moving Goodman forward,
nudging the world …

it's smooth, the dancers love its sound,
they're white, the lovers whirling round,
it's now, and better can't be found.

Wulf's Journey

Wulf maketh
preparation for his
journey

then he made up his mind
to visit the Abbey, leaving
his own dear Besse to twist
the flax and gather the bones.

First he made his way
to the water's edge, thick as it was
with vetches, lillies and herbs
and there summoned

terms agreed with
the bote maker

Blood-eye, the blind
boat maker who lived there
among the glittering frogs
and tail-less adders.

'Maken me an bote' Wulf said
'of herb and wasp nests
fastened with eye of fish
and Royal pitch'.

'Master I will,' he said,
straightening himself
like a wrought sword, like
a glottal tree.

'What must I render?'
said Wulf, 'three golden pins,
two stones from the shore, a dace
and nine withers.'

Night after night laboured
Blood-eye in his earth-sodden
byre to make and to finish
the boat

and by the day of the waif
its shape could be seen:
it glowed like a fleeing eel.
Then did Wulf seek out

and with Edgemon,
sword-maker

Edgemon, the deft, deaf
maker of blades
in his dark cavern
under the yearning cliffs.

'A blade shall ye maken for me',
'so I will, master, for you, for
payment of prayer for my father
and his, a noggin of pith and
a basin of scrawl.'

'Those you shall have', said Wulf,
on proof of its strength
and lightness of hold'.

he setteth forth on
the streyme

Then went forth Wulf, in his boat
on the stream, leaving all
he had known, trusting his boat
to convey him with safety.

Thus was his journey:

divers adversities

first, he encountered the
watery wolves. These
he dispatched with his
new-finished blade, then

did he find the teeth in the river,
their insidious grin, the dark
of their threats, but prayer
made them shudder and sink.

But grimmest of all were the serpents
which swam, under the waves,
in their silvery sheen, but these
he ignored, trusting the will of his boat.

his journey
continueth

And so he continued, by night
and by day, past monsters
and witches and tygers
and men in their fearsome
accouters, their accurate
spears in their hands, under
weather of lead or scorched
by the sun as if through a lens.

a vision of majestie

Now, as the boat
rounds a curve in the stream,
a vision of majesty, great
to behold

he reacheth his
destination

but which words cannot win
into verse. There,
Wulf ended his journey.

All But the Outcast

'Nature and Man' from 'Queen Mab', Shelley

Look on yonder earth:
The golden harvests spring; the unfailing sun
Sheds light and life; the fruits, the flowers, the trees,
Arise in due succession; all things speak
Peace, harmony and love

except earthquakes,
floods, disease, locusts and red-toothed,
red-clawed nature, bent at all costs
on unceasing replication. An ice age
waits in the wings for the next wobble.
The universe in nature's silent eloquence,
is silent. What can Man do but pretend?

Seventh Day

after Louis MacNeice, 'Sunday Morning'

Groggy from the night before,
you make your way to Tesco to pick up
Ragout, Lamb Biriani, Prosecco.
If you have time, you take the car
to be cleansed before you drive
Carol and the kids through sardined roads
to *The Packsaddle* for lunch. It's another
Sunday, but it's a day off at least.

Only the very elderly seem to hear the bells
which summon, whom to what?

Warm Valley

i.m. Ben Webster and Johnny Hodges

Smooth, soft, melodic as a nightingale, by increments
more forceful, taking the rhythm by its scruff, now
the roughest you ever heard, snorting and spluttering.

His smile the widest, his voice the gentlest, he cleans,
wipes and packs his instrument away and goes out
into the Harlem night. He'll take the case to his room.
He'll go and eat.

He bursts in
cane thrashing air –
beer, whiskey,
tumblers, glasses, bottles
explode off the bar

Hodges finds him, retrieves his coat and hat, his cane, leads him out
like a beast of burden. Finds him another bar where he can sob.

Rose of the Rio Grande

NBC broadcast: the Duke Ellington band at Eastwood Gardens,
Detroit, July 1940

Huskies yap, pull here, pull there,
leap, pull. Driver can't
hold. Yap, call, thrash, thrash. Tread on,
don't care, crunch, jump, pull, bump,
four legs, two, tails pound. Sledge
crunches, shifts, bark and whine,
sideways, upwards, tangle, slides,
clatter, rattle ...
                  forward
huskies, sledge, driver.
Yip! Yip! Onward, huskies!

There's such an ache in my heart

'I'll never be the same' recorded by Teddy Wilson
and Billie Holiday, 1937

The melody is stars, is birds,
is smiles that hide, is ache, …
but under it throbs heartbeat,
four to a bar, is 'I'm all that matters,
forget your birds and aching,
do your duty, *let love be King.*'

'No Chaos Dammit' (Jackson Pollock)

There's his pith helmet, his hand on top,
bobbing above the tall grass,
and there's his net, swishing in the air,
trying to catch, trying to catch ...
but all he catches is butterflies, insects, things.

Wheatfield with a Reaper

Van Gogh, 1899

no bells, no brakes,
children often,
dogs sometimes,
the cyclists of Amsterdam
run me down
twenty times a day.
Van Gogh saves me,
his wheatfield explosive,
his reaper distant.

The Lake

A seminar: *Ethics in Poetry*.
It was a coffee break and most people
were standing around chatting. I noticed
a girl sitting quietly on her own –
turned out she was ready to talk –
just needed someone to speak to her
and she was happy to open the book of her short life.

The last thing she talked about,
as we were brought to order for the next presentation,
was a lake – Tanganyika – where two white women had gone
with a black driver armed with a rifle.
When she was through with her studies
she would write poetry and this
would be her first. Her face lit up
as her imagination worked.

Africa, the savannah, the bumpy road,
crocodiles, the gun ... Hang on a minute,
you don't think I'd steal a poem from
a young poet just starting out do you?

To be fair though, she'd probably never know;
and it would be a different kind of poem anyway
to the one she'd write. You'll have to read
the next stanza if you want to find out if I did.

Heating and Plumbing

i.m. Ian Fyfe

The boiler was tired
but she would not have its silence,
its coldness, until he had gone.
So she held on, it held on, until,
lying beside her, he let go.

There were no darkened skies,
no exhalations whizzing in the air,
only an accidental metaphor
and the flare of a woman's grief.

The Neighbour's Cat

I hang out the clothes, I mow the lawn,
I read a book with a cup of tea. These,
are some of the things I do in the garden.
The trees are always there,
the grass is always there,
the fence to the right is always there,
the left side wall is always there,
as is next door's cat.

Not that I see it coming: I sense something,
look, and there it is, peering up,
its small, neat, pink, mouth
with its sharp white teeth making a sound
that sounds like a question, one
it hopes I can answer. It is soft
and almost bodiless when
I lift its small weight to set it on my lap.
I have no idea of it, nor does it, I suppose,
of me. But we are, for a moment, indivisible.

I hang the clothes, mow, drink tea.
The trees and grass are always there,
the fence and wall are always there,
as is a small absence.

One hundred years of

We're all in her room, looking at photos
of the long dead but very much alive.
They're all solemn, as though in awe of
the fleeting permanence of their moment.

This is a nice one: four children
in Sunday best, arranged by age:
Mum, Auntie Margaret, Uncle Doug,
and another girl – who would that be?

My mum's relaxed and cheerful these days,
a care home favourite, all darkness forgotten,
along with her husband's name, who we are
and where she is. Has she returned to some Eden?

I'm thinking of that other girl and linking her
with half-heard rumours. Was she
one of the memories my mum dumped
at the feet of the angels as she slipped past?

Lady with a Book

Vanessa Bell, 1945

Her hands rest on the open book.
But her gaze is on the wall opposite,
just above the skirting. It's
patterned in black twirls and spirals,
splashes of brown and grey,
a constellation of small explosions. She
will never be able to read a book again.

It's not just you

1. 'The possibilities of paint are never ending'

Frank Bowling, 2017

Dip your brush into that light. See what comes out:
Towards Crab Island; Sacha Jason Guyana Dreams;
Fishes, Wishes & Uncle Jack. Paint another –
call it *Silver Birch*, call it *No Man No Vote*.

Paint as 'an artist who happens to be black'. If they can't
see you in London go to New York – see how they
like you there. Go to Guyana. Find that light!

2. 'Gallant and distinguished service'

They were all white, and a long way from Guyana,
the tank crews whose 'valiant action' won that
Military Cross, won it for their Captain, Lord Carrington.

After the war they might have found employment
polishing it for him, holding it up, turning it
in their fingers in the sober English light.

Untitled

Lee Krasner: 'I am never free of the past'

Lena tree mirror Braque New Deal darkredwhite
Pollock pogrom Springs Accabonac crash assault
black flesh Paris Mondrian submerge Lenore Kelly-
green insomnia palingenesis umber fuschia-pink
biomorphic emerge Lee

The Red Rose

He brought her
a red rose,
a luscious, fresh,
red rose

which he forgot, which
he left on the soft carpet
in the warmth, becoming cool,
become cold
as the womb-car turned
to frozen hardness

and it became a frozen rose,
a frozen, shriveled rose,
retrieved
in the sharp morning light,
this limp, withered, rose,
this morning gift.

Underground Dog

A Collie, not very old,
head on the floor
among high heels, trainers,
white legs, black ones,
shopping bags, briefcases.

The lurching, screeching
train. The dog looking up,
settling again
on the shuddering floor.

All it needed to know,
this colour-blind dog,
was in its master's face.

Release

Sheffield.
Albert Terrace Road –
one hundred and nine.
Nastya
Kasia
Agnieszka
Weronika.

A man enters
and leaves
and another
and another.
As each comes out, he
looks both ways
turns left, towards
St Mary's Street –
Costa, betting shop, people, buses.
A man goes in
and leaves
and another

and John Hardcastle.
John and Weronika.
Weronika and John.
John comes out
looks left, turns right
towards Hope Street,
past the blue lamp, turns
past the blue lamp, turns
past the blue lamp, turns
and goes in.

Two Rivers Press has been publishing in and about Reading
since 1994. Founded by the artist Peter Hay (1951–2003),
the press continues to delight readers, local and further afield,
with its varied list of individually designed,
thought-provoking books.